⬤▬ IDENTIFYING TARGETED TRAINING NEEDS

A Practical Guide To
Beginning An Effective Training Strategy

Sally Sparhawk

Richard Chang Associates, Inc.
Publications Division
Irvine, California

IDENTIFYING TARGETED TRAINING NEEDS

A Practical Guide To Beginning An Effective Training Strategy

Sally Sparhawk

Library of Congress Catalog Card Number
94-68223

ISBN 1-883553-40-7

Richard Chang Associates, Inc.
Publications Division
41 Corporate Park, Suite 230
Irvine, CA 92714
(800) 756-8096 • Fax (714) 756-0853

RICHARD
CHANG
ASSOCIATES

ACKNOWLEDGMENTS

About The Author

Sally Sparhawk heads her own management and human resource development consulting firm, Sparhawk Consulting, based in Rochester, New York. Sally has over 20 years' experience in the human resource development field. Her expertise includes organizational development, development of training strategies, management of the training function, conducting needs analysis, and designing and developing customized training programs. She is a frequent speaker at national and international conferences sponsored by the American Society for Training and Development (ASTD).

The author would like to acknowledge the support of the entire team of professionals at Richard Chang Associates, Inc., for their contribution to the guidebook development process. In addition, special thanks are extended to the many client organizations who have helped us shape the practical ideas and proven methods shared in this guidebook.

Additional Credits

Editors: Marian Schickling and Joe Tinervia

Reviewer: P. Keith Kelly

Graphic Layout: Christina Slater

Cover Design: John Odam Design Associates

PREFACE

The 1990's have already presented individuals and organizations with some very difficult challenges to face and overcome. So who will have the advantage as we move toward the year 2000 and beyond?

The advantage will belong to those with a commitment to continuous learning. Whether on an individual basis or as an entire organization, one key ingredient to building a continuous learning environment is *The Practical Guidebook Collection* brought to you by the Publications Division of Richard Chang Associates, Inc.

After understanding the future *"learning needs"* expressed by our clients and other potential customers, we are pleased to publish *The Practical Guidebook Collection*. These guidebooks are designed to provide you with proven, *"real-world"* tips, tools, and techniques—on a wide range of subjects—that you can apply in the workplace and/or on a personal level immediately.

Once you've had a chance to benefit from *The Practical Guidebook Collection*, please share your feedback with us. We've included a brief *Evaluation and Feedback Form* at the end of the guidebook that you can fax to us at (714) 756-0853.

With your feedback, we can continuously improve the resources we are providing through the Publications Division of Richard Chang Associates, Inc.

Wishing you successful reading,

Richard Y. Chang
President and CEO
Richard Chang Associates, Inc.

TABLE OF CONTENTS

"Before everything else, getting ready is the secret of success."

Henry Ford

CHAPTER ONE

INTRODUCTION

The business world is changing rapidly, and it seems as if we are all running to keep up. Everyone is being asked to stretch—to do more than ever before—and to do it faster. In general, employees are more than willing to answer the call; but to do so effectively, they need information—information on how to tackle their demanding, new responsibilities.

One of the new responsibilities you may be asked to tackle is training. Perhaps you will simply be asked to coach another employee, or you may be asked to facilitate a formal or an informal training session for your group, or you may find yourself responsible for an entire training project. Whatever your particular situation, you will need help, especially if you haven't had any formal instruction in training others.

On the other hand, you may be an experienced trainer who is looking for ways to increase the impact of your efforts within your organization. Individual contributions are being closely assessed by management, and everyone is looking for effective ways to demonstrate value to the organization. There are a number of effective techniques you can use within the training process to achieve greater recognition and add value to the organization.

Why Read This Guidebook?

This guidebook simplifies the process of identifying your training needs. In a step-by-step process, it explains what you need to do to define the training need and develop a plan for addressing it. It also provides worksheets you can use on the job to keep you headed in the right direction.

The design of this guidebook is strictly *"no frills."* The information you need to get up and running with your training project is presented clearly, concisely, and in a nontechnical way. *(You have enough to do without worrying about the finer points of training jargon.)*

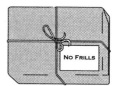

In addition, examples have been included to demonstrate how each step relates to a real-world situation. You can use this book to learn or strengthen your training skills and at the same time expand your role and credibility within your organization.

Who Should Read This Guidebook?

This guidebook has broad appeal. You will definitely benefit from it if:

☑ You've been asked to do a training needs analysis, and you're not even sure what one is

☑ You're in charge of developing training for your group, and the only training you've ever done is teaching your dog to sit

☑ You've got a training project to do, and the last one you did was 6 years ago

☑ You've just been made head of the training group, and you're not sure your 10 years' experience as a chemist in the research department has adequately prepared you for this new responsibility

How am I to going to conduct a needs analysis?

In short, you should read this guidebook if you fall into any of the following groups:

The Rank Beginners. Also known in various parts of the country as rookies, novices, or tenderfoots, these people have little or no formal or informal education in training theory and application but nonetheless have been given the responsibility to conduct a training needs assessment or develop training materials.

The Moderately Experienced. Affectionately known as survivors, these people have been involved in a training project at some point in their careers but could use a refresher course before plunging in again.

The Veterans. As *"pros,"* these people have extensive experience in doing training projects, but the business world is changing under their feet, and they can use this guidebook to learn new strategies for success and to learn how to position their training groups for the demands of the future.

This is not, of course, an exhaustive list of candidates for this guidebook. It is actually only a list of those who might have a direct need for the information it contains. A second group, those who have an indirect need for the information, could also benefit from reading it.

If you are a supervisor or a manager, who has assigned training responsibilities to a member of your staff, read this guidebook to understand the process your employee will be using. Then, give the guidebook *(appropriately annotated)* to your employee as a gesture of your support for the activities to be undertaken.

This guidebook also makes an excellent tool for coaching others in the training process. Whether you are coaching line personnel to do a training task or developing new training personnel, the step-by-step approach will facilitate your efforts and make the process of doing a training needs analysis understandable to others.

When And How To Use It

You are the best judge of how you can use this guidebook to meet your training needs. Here are a few suggestions:

☑ As a life preserver, to keep you afloat as you navigate your way through your first training project. The worksheets at the end of each chapter will help you identify the necessary steps and organize the individual tasks.

☑ As a refresher course, to help you recall your own unique process and to broaden your approach.

☑ As a resource, for helping others learn, or for ideas for managing the training process in a changing business environment.

No matter what your reason for turning to this guidebook, you will find the support and information you need to successfully identify your training needs.

CHAPTER TWO

DETERMINING YOUR TRAINING NEEDS

Andy was the manager of order processing, and he had a problem. He was not satisfied with the performance of his group. They seemed to be taking forever to process essential paperwork through the department. He decided that a time-management training program would solve the problem.

Andy hired an outside vendor to come in and present a full-day time-management course to his staff. All 14 people on the staff attended. The evaluations indicated that the course had been well received and that the information contained in the course had been helpful to the staff.

After the course, Andy happily anticipated a change in the speed of processing paperwork. Unfortunately, it never happened. The paperwork continued to be processed at the same snail-slow pace. Andy was completely dismayed; he had spent over $4,000 on the time management course, and he wasn't getting the results he expected. What had gone wrong?

Andy made a classic business mistake: He selected and shot his arrow *(time-management training)* before he set up his target, and thus he aimed his solution into the void. What you get out of a void is nothing; and that's exactly what Andy got—for $4,000.

What Is A Needs Analysis?

If Andy had targeted his training needs by gathering and analyzing information about the situation before he decided what the cause of it was, he could have avoided this disaster. If he had taken the time to determine his training needs, he would have discovered exactly what was needed to address the issue. This investigation, sometimes referred to as a needs analysis or a needs assessment, enables you to gather enough information to identify the situation and understand how to correct it.

Your needs analysis gives you vital information to assure you accurately hit the target.

It tells you where the target is

You may suspect that the problem exists within your own area, as Andy did, but a needs analysis might indicate that the problem extends beyond your group. For example, if you are having difficulty improving your cycle-time for a product, the issue might include your manufacturing process; but it might also include the engineering or the packaging and shipping department as well. A needs analysis expands your view and helps you pinpoint all targets.

It tells you how large the target is

Maybe your process improvement challenges are the result of your people not knowing how to properly run a new machine, or maybe the challenge is an organizationwide quality issue. Your needs analysis will tell you how big the solution needs to be.

It tells you how far away the target is

Perhaps you only need to teach your group better telephone skills to address the problem—or maybe you need a more sophisticated telephone system to handle the increased demand. Your needs analysis will give you these answers.

It tells you what kind of arrows to use

Training comes in several different shapes and sizes. Your needs analysis will help you determine whether you need to do coaching, small group training, large group training, computer-based training, or any combination of these and other options.

It tells you who should shoot the arrows

Once you determine the training need, you consider the best way to meet it. For instance, if you need to do team-building, it might be best to use internal line managers as trainers because they are part of the team. You might also want to consider using the training department's instructors. In some cases, an external resource would best suit your needs. The information you gather for the needs analysis helps you make this decision.

It tells you when to shoot

Timing is everything. Some training is best given immediately, such as new employee safety procedures. Other training, such as learning a new computer system, may best be given just before the new system is installed or perhaps immediately after it is installed so training participants can practice as they learn. Training linked to company initiatives may best be presented in a package with other company issues. Your needs analysis can give you vital information about the best time to present the training.

It warns you about crosscurrents

Office politics is the wind shear of any organizational effort. If you expect to hit the target after you identify it, you have to be knowledgeable about how these crosscurrents will affect your arrow's trajectory. Then you can adjust your stance, your equipment, or your attitude to compensate.

You should also keep a weather-eye out for entrenched opinions about your group or other groups. If turf issues exist, you can bet they will surface just as you are taking aim. You need to deal with these situations as part of your needs analysis work. Clear the air so that nothing stands between you and a successful hit on the target.

Why Do A Needs Analysis?

The most important reason for doing a needs analysis is to assure that your training addresses your situation. It is both costly and embarrassing to recommend a direction that has no impact on the issue.

Even an informal needs analysis would have saved Andy a lot of time, money, and face. Consider what might have happened if Andy had done a needs analysis instead of assuming he knew the issue.

Andy begins by observing his staff in action and talking to his key players. He uncovers two important facts:

> ☐ His staff doesn't know how to use the computer software very well.
>
> ☐ The forms they use to input information into the computer are in a different order from what is asked for on the computer screen.

Andy has the forms redesigned to align with the software program. He also brings in a software expert to answer questions and demonstrate the most efficient way to use the program. Now, the customer orders fly through the department like Robin Hood's arrows.

Summary

Determining your training needs is the first step on the path to effective training. When you do a needs analysis, you focus your attention on the target and identify the means for getting there. The needs analysis process also involves others and helps them understand the issues you are all facing. Involvement builds commitment, and those who helped you start the process form a cadre of support as you continue down the path to a solution.

For the more pragmatic, there are three essential reasons for doing a needs analysis:

☑ To ensure your solution addresses the issue

☑ To effectively focus your resources, time, and effort toward a targeted training solution

☑ To eliminate the necessity of having to look for another job

If any of these reasons appeals to you, you will find more detailed information on how to effectively target your training needs on the following pages.

CHAPTER THREE

PLANNING YOUR TRAINING PROJECT

Identifying your training needs is the first step in a larger training process that takes you from your initial inquiries all the way to delivery and evaluation of the final training package. This training process is called the High-IMPACT Training™ Model.

Understanding The High-IMPACT Training Model

The High-IMPACT Training Model is a six-phase process that focuses on providing effective, targeted training. If you follow this model, your training efforts will have a positive impact on your organization.

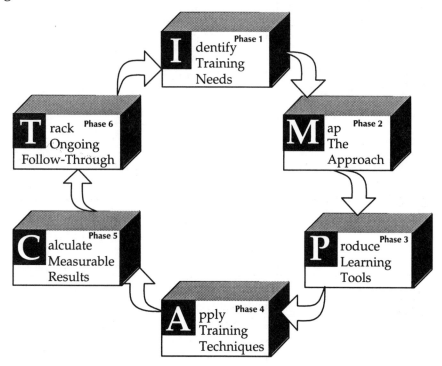

Using The High-IMPACT Training Model

Each phase of the High-IMPACT Training Model moves your training project forward. To use the model effectively, you should complete each phase in order. The product of each phase is the raw material for the next phase.

The following table illustrates your activities in each phase and the product you will be producing.

PHASE	ACTION	PRODUCT
1. **I**dentify **Training Needs**	Gather and analyze appropriate information	A description of the specific training needed to improve job performance
2. **M**ap The **Approach**	Define what needs to be learned to improve job performance Choose the appropriate training approach	Detailed objectives for the training program A design plan for the training program
3. **P**roduce **Learning Tools**	Create the actual training materials	Training manuals Facilitator's guide Audiovisual aids Job aids Etc.
4. **A**pply Training **Techniques**	Deliver the training as designed to ensure successful results	Instructor-led training Computer-based training One-on-one coaching, etc.
5. **C**alculate **Measurable Results**	Assess whether your training/coaching accomplished actual performance improvement; communicate the results, and redesign (*if needed*)	An evaluation report A redesigned course, if needed
6. **T**rack Ongoing **Follow-Through**	Ensure that the impact of the training does not diminish	Ongoing suggestions and ideas that support the training

The High-IMPACT Training Model is a valuable tool for guiding your training development efforts. Each phase is designed to focus your activities for maximum results.

Phase 1: Identify Training Needs

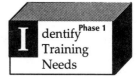

This phase *(the subject of this guidebook)* uncovers the specific training needed to improve job performance. You investigate the reasons the training is needed and describe the training you must develop to answer the need.

Phase 2: Map the Training Approach

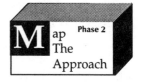

Once you have identified in Phase 1 the training needed, you are ready to develop measurable objectives for the training and map out a design plan. The objectives define exactly what the training should accomplish and provide a means for measuring its success. To develop the design plan, you use the objectives for guidance and prepare an outline for the training that will meet the objectives.

Phase 3: Produce Effective Learning Tools

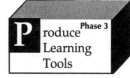

This phase involves the actual development of the specific training approach you have chosen. It might include a training manual or materials to support on-the-job training, or it might be an instructor-led course, or it might be something completely different. You may develop the needed materials yourself or work with others to develop them. The objectives and design plan from Phase 2 guide the development of these training materials.

Phase 4: Apply Successful Training Techniques

In this phase, you deliver the training to those who need it. If it is an instructor-led course, you actually run the course with students. If you developed job aids to use on the job, then in this phase you try them out with those who will use them. Whatever training was developed in Phase 3 is introduced in Phase 4 to those who need it.

Phase 5: Calculate Measurable Results

In this phase, you review the objectives developed in Phase 2 and determine whether the training is achieving them. Now you see why measurable objectives are so important. You can now look at the specific measures for success that you identified in Phase 2 and see if they have been achieved.

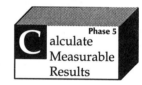

Phase 6: Track Ongoing Follow-Through

If Phase 5 confirms that you have created a successful training effort, don't rest on your laurels. You have a responsibility to ensure that the training continues to be effective. Change is constant in organizations, and you must respond to changes that affect your training efforts by continuing to implement suggestions and ideas that support the existing training materials and programs.

Use this guidebook to accomplish the first phase in the High-IMPACT Training Model—Identify Targeted Training Needs. Other guidebooks in this series address the other phases in the Model.

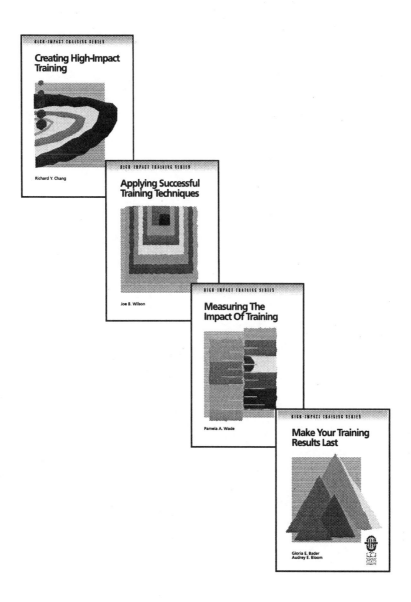

PLANNING YOUR NEEDS ANALYSIS

You are a lot luckier than poor Andy. You know that there is a logical process for doing an entire training project. You know that this High-IMPACT Training Model has six phases that, if properly executed, ensure a successful training impact.

In skipping the first phase, Identify Targeted Training Needs, Andy leaped to a solution without determining the real issue. In fact, the solution to his problem was just as much a mystery to him at the end of his process as it was at the beginning.

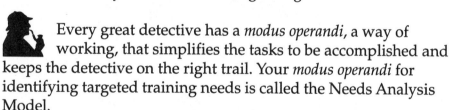

When you do a needs analysis to target your training needs, you become a detective solving a mystery: Which target is the right one? There are plenty of targets out there you could hit with your solution (*Andy's solution was time-management training*), but the idea is to identify and then hit the right target.

Every great detective has a *modus operandi*, a way of working, that simplifies the tasks to be accomplished and keeps the detective on the right trail. Your *modus operandi* for identifying targeted training needs is called the Needs Analysis Model.

Using The Six Steps Of The Needs Analysis Model

The Needs Analysis Model summarizes the actions necessary to complete the first phase of the High-IMPACT Training Model— Identify Targeted Training Needs.

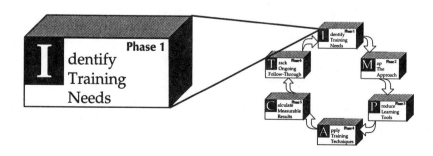

Like the High-IMPACT Training Model, the Needs Analysis Model has six actions you take to create six related products. These six actions are:

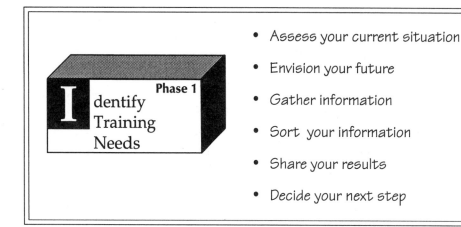

- Assess your current situation
- Envision your future
- Gather information
- Sort your information
- Share your results
- Decide your next step

Each of these actions will be discussed in detail in the following chapters. When you have completed all six actions, you will know what the issue is and have a plan to address it. That information is the starting point for the second phase of the High-IMPACT Training Model—Map the Approach. This building-block approach ensures that you have a strong foundation on which to build your training solution.

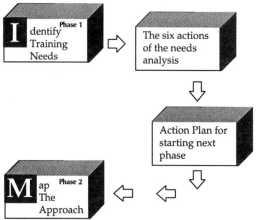

Each action of the needs analysis is driven by a question which focuses your attention and results in a concrete product that helps you achieve the next step in the process. These focusing questions and the end products that result from them are shown on the follc ving chart:

ACTION NEEDED	QUESTIONS TO ASK	END PRODUCT
1. Assess your current situation	Where are we now?	A clear definition of the situation
2. Envision your future	Where do we want to be?	A clear description of what the future would look like if the correct actions were taken
3. Gather information	What do we need to know?	A systematic gathering of relevant ideas and information from appropriate people to establish the whole picture
4. Sort your information	What does this information tell us?	Themes and issues that need to be addressed
5. Share your results	How do we use this information to move forward?	A summary of issues and recommendations
6. Decide your next step	What actions should we take to have impact?	Action Plan for beginning Phase 2, Map the Training Approach

Developing A Strategy For Success

Although the six actions of the Needs Analysis Model are
sequential, it may be helpful to look at the model as a target.

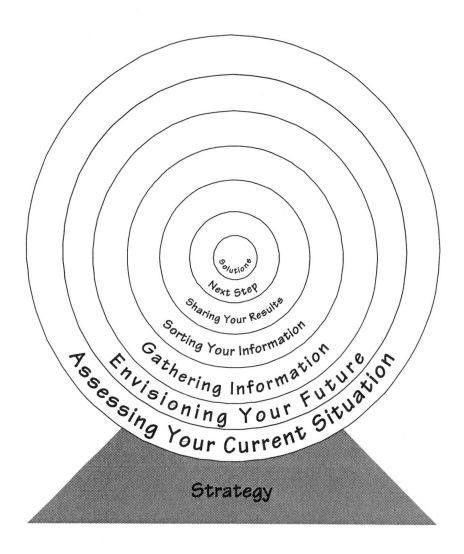

Each ring of the target represents an action you take to move you
closer to your solution. Notice that the base of this target is labeled
"*strategy.*" Without strategy, to support it, your target would fall flat
and be extremely difficult to hit.

With an effective strategy, your target is:

☑ Visible, to you and to others in the organization

☑ Solid, braced by clear thinking and logical planning

☑ Achievable, with a steady aim

An effective training strategy involves three elements:

☑ Establish a partnership with others

☑ Consider the larger picture

☑ Serve the customer

Establish a partnership with others

Conducting a needs analysis should never be a lonely process. If you want to ensure that you get the information you need, you will have to involve other people in the process.

People love to be asked what they think. If they believe you will seriously consider their contributions, they will offer you all kinds of useful information. Each person that you involve in your needs analysis becomes a partner in shaping the solution. Keep them all informed, and they will become your support group for implementing the solution.

Consider which individuals in your organization are critical to the success of your needs analysis—and then enlist their help. For example, it could be good strategy to involve your boss and others in management who will ultimately be asked to approve your training approach. You should involve those who will be the recipients of the training. Ask for their opinions, and keep them informed about your activities. In this way, they will understand what you are trying to achieve and why.

Consider the larger picture

Since your group is not working in a vacuum, you should consider how your training challenge is affecting other groups in the organization. For example, if you are creating a product that is passed to another group, how would that group be affected by changes in your methods that might come about when you implement your solution? How do they see your training issue? In fact, you might ask yourself if, in defining your issue, you have looked beyond your own needs. Overlooking others' needs might doom your solution. Expanding the boundaries of your needs analysis to include those outside your group is one strategy for seeing the larger picture.

While you are looking at the larger picture, take some time to consider the needs of the organization as a whole. Linking your training solution directly to the business goals of the organization is an excellent strategy. Study your organization's mission, vision, and business objectives. Then consider how the achievement of your training solution supports one or more of these objectives.

Job security is definitely enhanced when you make a conscious effort to help the organization achieve its objectives. No longer is achieving organization objectives the sole responsibility of upper management. In the current business environment, everyone is expected to contribute to the organization's goals. Those who embrace this idea and actually tie their contributions directly to the organization direction will be well positioned, well thought of— and, possibly, even well rewarded.

Serve the customer

In the heat of meeting everyone else's needs, don't forget your customers. Your ultimate training solution should benefit them as well. In thinking of your customers' needs, remember that you have two different types of customer:

- ☐ External customers who pay hard cash for the products or services of your organization, and

- ☐ Internal customers, who work within your organization, receive *"product"* from you, and add their value to it before it reaches the external customers.

Ask yourself how your actions fit into the chain of serving your customers. How are you adding value for them? Andy helped his external customers by speeding up the processing of their orders through his department. He also helped his internal customers by getting them the paperwork they needed more quickly.

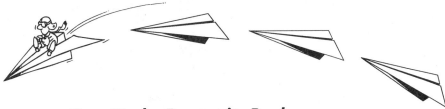

Case Study: Prosperity Bank

Like all smart companies, Prosperity Bank is concerned about its future. The aggressive marketing tactics of its competitors have affected Prosperity's profits. To increase its profitability, Prosperity has asked its Telephone Customer Service Department (TCSD) to sell bank services when customers call with questions or concerns. Natalie works in TCSD and has been successful at increasing sales through her customer interactions. Unfortunately, most of the other customer service representatives have not been as successful. Petra, Natalie's manager, asks Natalie to investigate the situation and determine what training needs to be done to improve the sales performance of the other customer service reps.

Natalie is delighted to help her group but a little nervous about doing this needs analysis. She has no formal training experience. Luckily, she has a copy of this guidebook and plans to use it as a *"life preserver."*

Summary

Anyone can follow the steps of a needs analysis and come out with an adequate solution. But a solution that is truly targeted and effective requires the application of strategy.

Good strategy requires that you align your training activities with your organization's direction. To do this, you must be familiar with the mission, vision, and business objectives of your organization. You also need to establish partnerships, consider the larger picture, and serve the customer.

Raising your sights from your own needs and seeing how the needs of your associates, your organization as a whole, and your customers relate to your issue assure you of a truer aim.

By involving others in the needs analysis process, you enlist supporters for the solution and communicate your efforts to a larger audience. And by considering the needs of your customers, you demonstrate an understanding of the mission of your organization and ensure customer satisfaction with your solution.

With your strategy in place, you are ready to proceed to the individual steps of the needs analysis.

CHAPTER FOUR WORKSHEET:
USING STRATEGY TO CONTRIBUTE TO
ORGANIZATION GROWTH

Use the following questions to guide your strategy for identifying targeted training needs.

The Larger Picture

1. What is the mission of your organization? What is its purpose for existing?

_____

_____

_____

_____

_____

2. What is the vision of your organization? Where does your organization want to go?

_____

_____

_____

_____

_____

_____

3. What are the business objectives of your organization?

_____

_____

_____

_____

_____

_____

_____

_____

Working in Partnership

4. What other areas or departments do you interact with?

_____

_____

_____

_____

_____

_____

_____

_____

5. Whom should you involve? Who is critical to your success?

_____

_____

_____

_____

_____

_____

_____

_____

Serving the Customer

6. Who are your internal and external customers?

_____

_____

_____

_____

_____

_____

_____

_____

ASSESSING YOUR CURRENT SITUATION

In a needs analysis, assessing your current situation provides a clear definition of the problem. All of your other actions in the needs analysis depend on your making this assessment accurately. It is a very important first step.

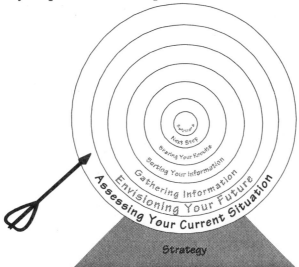

To get a complete picture of your current situation, ask yourself these three questions:

☐ Where are we now?

☐ Why do we think we need training?

☐ What organization issues are driving the need for training?

Where Are We Now?

Begin your needs analysis by exploring the current situation. Start by noting what you already know about your situation. Consider asking others in the group to define the current situation as they see it. Involving others right from the start is a good way to begin establishing a partnership for the whole process.

The emphasis in defining your current situation is on capturing a description of where you are right now. As you do this, however, you may begin to see potential solutions to your situation or you may get ideas from others on what to do about the situation. Jot these ideas down to use later as you gather and analyze information; but for right now, focus on just describing your starting point.

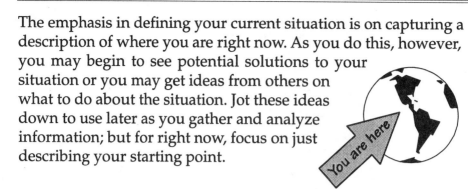

 **Andy's assessment...**
of his current situation was that the paperwork was slow. This was an accurate assessment, but since Andy didn't go on to the other actions of an effective needs analysis, he never discovered that there were other factors contributing to the paperwork delay....

Why Do We Think We Need Training?

The obvious answer to this is, *"We need training to address the situation."* But ask yourself, *"Why now?"* Think about what is going on in your department right now. Is there a history behind this situation? What is the issue, problem, or situation that is creating the need or demand for this training?

Perhaps your department is responding to pressure from upper management to improve cycle-time or quality, or perhaps, like Prosperity Bank, outside competition is driving the need. Whatever the reason, it is an important part of your assessment of the current situation.

Don't try to answer this question without getting ideas from others. Your perspective on the situation is not the only one; and if you miss vital information right here at the beginning of the process, you could derail yourself and your project.

Remember Andy: When he thought about why training was needed, he determined that it would speed up the process. He didn't ask others what they thought. As a result, he completely misread the situation and took off down a path that led nowhere.

What Organization Issues Are Driving The Need For Training?

This question draws you into the larger picture that should be a part of your overall strategy. If you know the mission, vision, and business objectives of your organization, you should be able to determine what is going on in your organization that is driving the need for training.

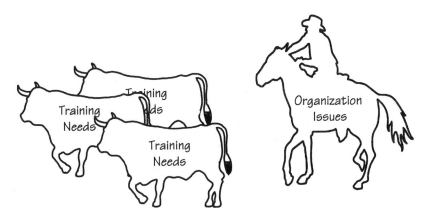

Again, others can help you with this process. Your direct management can provide insights into the importance of your task. Don't hesitate to probe for this type of information. Others may also provide useful information about events that are not currently driving the training need but which might have an impact on your situation, such as expected mergers or personnel changes.

Even if your management doesn't have any additional information to contribute, asking involves management in your project. That in itself is a good idea. Management's involvement now could translate into support later in the process.

Working alone, Andy went ahead with just his own knowledge of the situation—with disastrous results. He didn't address the right situation, and he lost credibility with his management and his staff. Obviously, Andy is a poor role model for identifying targeted training needs. Let's see how Natalie at Prosperity Bank handles the task of identifying training needs.

Prosperity Bank: The Balance Sheet

Natalie's manager, Petra, has asked Natalie to start a project to plan for training all the customer service reps to sell bank services in addition to their current responsibility of answering customer questions and requests. Natalie begins by asking her manager what the current situation is. Petra thinks about it for a minute and then says: *"Sales just haven't been what we in management thought they would be. The customer service reps talk to hundreds of customers every day, and yet our sales have gone up only slightly since we started this new effort. Even though we gave everyone sales training, overall performance is not improving. Maybe they don't know the products well enough; maybe they need more sales training. I don't know. You have the best sales on the team. That's why I'm asking you to look at the situation and tell me what you think we need. If we could have some plans by next month, that would really help."*

Petra's information is very helpful to Natalie for assessing the current situation. It is clear that Petra has thought about the situation very carefully. Natalie decides Petra is probably a good source for more initial information. She asks her, *"Why do you think we need the training now?"*

Petra explains: *"There are a number of reasons why we feel it is important to move forward on this training right now. First of all, there is more competition in town from banks with lower rates, and we don't want to lose customers to them simply because our customers don't know what services we can offer them. Also, management believes retail business has more profit potential for the bank and is focusing effort there."*

Natalie is curious to know why her group has been selected to increase sales. In the past, the customer service reps responded to customer needs, and Natalie knows some of her coworkers are uncomfortable with *"selling"* to customers.

Petra understands Natalie's concerns, but Petra points out: *"The customer service reps already have contact with a large number of our customers. The reps are in a good position to hear about customer needs and respond to them. There is also a similar effort going on in the branches with tellers and customer service and sales reps."*

To address the question about organization issues that might be affecting the request for training, Natalie gets more information about the company mission, vision, and goals. She discovers that this effort is part of the organization's goal to provide better service to customers and more profitability for shareholders. If the bank is going to meet the year-end targets, this and several other initiatives will need to be successful.

Natalie makes a chart of all the information she has gathered about the current situation.

Where are we now?	Sales are lagging behind projections. Performance has not improved as a result of sales training. Natalie represents level of sales results desired. Customer reps have direct contact with customers. Branches are being asked to increase sales.
Why do we think we need training?	More competition. Retail business is being targeted by management for more revenue.
What organization issues are driving the need for training?	Improve customer service. Provide more profitability for shareholders.

Notice that Natalie's chart includes information from Petra and information that Natalie knew herself. It is the combination that provides a powerful picture of the current situation at Prosperity Bank.

Natalie is off to a very good start with her needs analysis. She has gathered enough information to understand what the current situation is, why it is important to do the training now, and how the training will influence her organization's objectives.

Natalie has also used excellent strategy in this initial effort. She has formed a partnership with Petra by asking for her input. She has also looked at the larger picture so she can consider the needs of the organization and the customer in her project results.

At this point, Natalie could go on to the next action of the needs analysis—envisioning the future—or she could continue to ask the three key questions of others in the organization who might be able to provide additional information for her assessment of the current situation. She has decided to go on.

Summary

Knowing when you have the right amount of information to describe your current situation requires common sense. If you have made a conscientious attempt to describe what you know and to ask others for their opinions, then you can feel comfortable with the results. Most needs analyses have a short timeline, so you don't have the luxury of absolute certainty at this stage. At some point, you must decide you have enough of a description and move on. You will gather more information along the way.

CHAPTER FIVE WORKSHEET:
CAPTURING YOUR ASSESSMENT
OF THE CURRENT SITUATION

1. Where are we now? *(Describe the current situation that has prompted the needs analysis.)*

_____

_____

_____

2. Why do we think we need training? *(What is the business need?)*

_____

_____

_____

_____

3. What organization issues either are driving the need for training or will have an impact on our situation?

_____

_____

_____

_____

ENVISIONING YOUR FUTURE

Envisioning your future is defining and understanding what your group will look like after the training has been accomplished. When you think about how the future would look if your training efforts were successful, you often discover aspects of your vision that have nothing to do with training but are critical to the success of your efforts. It is important to uncover these elements early in the needs analysis so that they can be fully addressed as well.

To create your vision, ask yourself these three questions:

☆ Where do we want to be?   ☆ What would success look like?

☆ Do we have the whole picture?

Where Do We Want To Be?

Imagination is a powerful tool for changing the world. All great inventors and leaders call on their imaginations to see what has never been and to inspire commitment and progress. They often don't know how they are going to get to the future, but they already have a clear picture of what it will look like.

Your own organization's vision is an example of dreaming the future. The business objectives *(developed after the vision has been defined)* are the steps to get there. You use the same process in your needs analysis. You define the future and then you identify the action steps to get you there.

Just as you carefully developed a description of your current situation, you must now develop an equally careful description of the future. Use your imagination to see your group as it would be if the issues of the current situation were successfully addressed.

Don't worry about how you are going to get to this future state right now; that's what the complete needs analysis will tell you. Just imagine where you would like to be.

What Would Success Look Like?

To get a clear idea of your future, think about what your group would look like if things were working right. What would be different if the issue were resolved successfully?

Think about how the solution would help the customer and your entire organization. Specifically, what benefits would they get if your dream of the future came true?

An excellent way to measure the future is to determine if there are any quantifiable numbers that would indicate success. In a

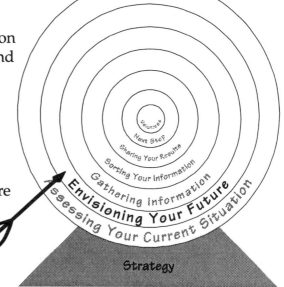

production area, for instance, successful training might result in, say, a 20 percent increase in productivity or a specific reduction in defects per one hundred thousand units manufactured. If numbers or measures are important to your success, include them in your description of the future.

Do We Have The Whole Picture?

When we dream of the future, we tend to dream of the fulfillment of our own needs; but in an organization, we are not alone. Your vision of the future must consider the needs of others. Think about how you would interact with others outside your group in your future state. How would your solution benefit the organization as a whole? How will it benefit the customer?

This line of thinking can uncover some of the challenges of getting to that desired future state. When you broaden the picture, you may discover that a successful training solution involves more than just addressing the training issues. You may discover other issues, not under your direct control, that must be resolved as well.

Enlarging the picture also reveals key players outside your group whose involvement may be essential to the success of your needs analysis. You may discover areas of support you can tap to strengthen your results. By identifying others who have a stake in the success of your project, you expand your resources and increase your chances of success.

Prosperity Bank: Investing In The Future

With a clear understanding of her current situation, Natalie begins the second action of her needs analysis—envisioning the future. To get Petra's vision of the future, Natalie asks her what she thinks the training will accomplish.

Petra says: "*Ideally, when a customer calls about a problem with a monthly state-ment, the rep would be able to address that problem and then probe to understand the customer's financial concerns. Since the customers call us for service, we may be able to help them understand what their needs are and how our services could help them.*"

Natalie then asks Petra to define what success would look like. She asks Petra, *"What would be different if we are successful?"* Petra replies: *"Some reps have been selling services for years, but it has been more by chance than by plan. Management has set a goal for us this year of a 30 percent increase in sales. I think we can do even better than that, but at this point, we have only a 10 percent increase."* To ensure that she has the whole picture, Natalie asks Petra about the other departments they work with and how things might be different there too. Petra replies: *"It would be great if we had more advance information from marketing about new products or services. It would also be great if operations worked better with us to serve the customers in a more timely fashion."*

Natalie is satisfied with the information she has gathered about the future. She makes a chart to summarize her progress:

Where do we want to be?	Reps easily move from customer concerns to customer needs Reps assist customers in understanding how our services could help them
What would success look like?	A minimum 30% increase in sales by year-end Reps comfortable with "selling" to customers
Do we have the whole picture?	Need advance information on new products/services from marketing Need operations to work better with us to serve customers

Summary

When you envision the future, you continue to use the three elements of a strategic needs analysis. Specifically, you:

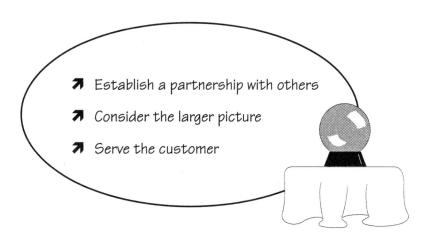

➚ Establish a partnership with others

➚ Consider the larger picture

➚ Serve the customer

By asking others what they think the training will accomplish, you continue to expand your partnership and gain their interest and commitment. When you consider how your vision of the future will affect others, including your customers, you fulfill the other two elements of a strategic needs analysis.

You may find it helpful to use Natalie's method of documenting the key points of each step of the needs analysis. Stopping to capture the key facts of each action helps you refresh your memory about where you are and where you are going. It also provides you with a document you can share with others to show progress and keep everyone focused on the target.

CHAPTER SIX WORKSHEET:
YOUR DREAM FOR THE FUTURE

1. Where do we want to be?

_____

_____

_____

_____

2. What would success look like?

_____

_____

_____

_____

3. Do we have the whole picture?

_____

_____

_____

_____

4. What are the supports for getting the desired results?

_____

_____

_____

_____

5. What are the challenges to getting the desired results?

_____

_____

_____

_____

_____

6. Whom do we need to involve or convince to get the desired results?

_____

_____

_____

_____

_____

GATHERING INFORMATION

The first two actions of your needs analysis:

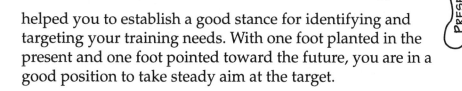

- ↗ Assessing the current situation

- ↗ Envisioning the future

helped you to establish a good stance for identifying and targeting your training needs. With one foot planted in the present and one foot pointed toward the future, you are in a good position to take steady aim at the target.

But before you shoot, you have to know where you are aiming. The next three steps in the needs analysis process:

- ↗ Gathering information,

- ↗ Sorting your information, and

- ↗ Sharing your results

help you define what you are aiming at. In the information-gathering step, you are collecting information to better understand what needs to be done to reach your future state. You are investigating to discover:

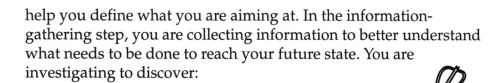

- ↗ The needs and perceptions of others

- ↗ What barriers must be overcome

- ↗ Your group's current skills, knowledge, and attitudes

- ↗ What skills, knowledge, and attitudes are needed for the future

- ↗ What needs to be done and how to do it

The information-gathering step is an opportunity for you to collect raw data from whatever sources you feel would be helpful. The three concerns of gathering information are:

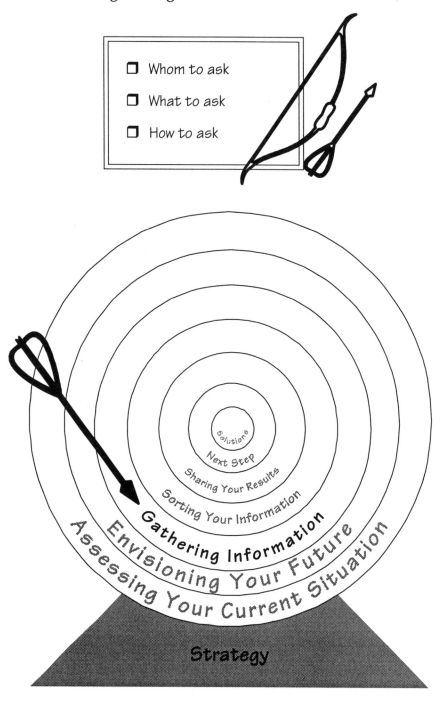

☐ Whom to ask

☐ What to ask

☐ How to ask

Solutions

Next Step

Sharing Your Results

Sorting Your Information

Gathering Information

Envisioning Your Future

Assessing Your Current Situation

Strategy

Whom To Ask

There are two aspects of this issue. You must decide:

☐ Whom will you select to answer your questions?

☐ Who will *do* the asking?

Whom will you select to answer your questions?

In selecting individuals or groups to provide information, ask yourself these questions:

☐ Who knows the most about the situation?

☐ Who wants to be involved?

☐ Who would have a different perspective?

☐ Who could be critical to the success of the project?

☐ Who might have good ideas to share?

☐ Who can provide objective information?

If possible, seek suggestions about potential contributors of information from those you have already involved in your project. Try to maintain a balance of participants. The list should be representative of those affected by the outcome. If possible, include employees, management, and both internal and external customers. One way to ensure a balance is to make a chart of the areas you want to include and the job levels to consider and then fill in the names of possible contributors using the questions to guide you.

POSSIBLE CONTRIBUTORS

	ENGINEERING	SHOP FLOOR	SHIPPING	OTHER INTERESTED PARTIES
EMPLOYEES	Lydia Gus Danielle Chelsey	Tamika Ali Tim Anna	Miranda Van Gene Sandy	Customers (large and small)
SUPERVISORS	Lynn	Tony	Cody	Sales manager
MANAGERS	Leo	Ashley	Andre	VP of division

Once the chart is complete, you can select individuals or groups from each area and job level to create a representative sample. Make sure you end up with a true cross section—some from each column and row.

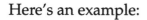

Here's an example:

SELECTED CONTRIBUTORS

	ENGINEERING	SHOP FLOOR	SHIPPING	OTHER INTERESTED PARTIES
EMPLOYEES	Lydia Gus Danielle Chelsey	Tamika Ali Tim Anna	Miranda Van Gene Sandy	Customers (large and small)
SUPERVISORS	Lynn	Tony	Cody	Sales manager
MANAGERS	Leo	Ashley	Andre	VP of division

You should also check for balance between long-term and short-term employees, male and female employees, union and nonunion employees, or whatever other categories are important for a fair selection process in your organization.

Who will do the asking?

Selecting information gatherers is another opportunity to involve others in your project. Key players might welcome the chance to participate in interviews, focus groups, and surveys as information gatherers.

Consider the following questions when selecting information gatherers:

☐ Who can remain objective?

☐ Who wants to be an information gatherer?

☐ Who can take the time to do it?

☐ Whose involvement would increase the chances of success?

☐ Who has strong communication and interpersonal skills?

☐ Who has experience in facilitating groups?

What To Ask

Explain to participants the purpose of the needs analysis and share with them the desired future state. Don't be surprised if they want to add details to the future-state description. Determining the right approach is an evolving process in a needs analysis, and information comes to you at every step of the way. If the information is valuable, incorporate it, and keep moving forward.

Be sure to stress the importance of individual contributions to the success of the needs analysis. The more open and welcoming you are to comments, the more information you will get to direct your aim.

The questions to include in information gathering should address your situation and your desired future state. You are the best judge of what questions you should ask.

Here are a few suggestions to get you started:

☐ How do you see the situation?

☐ What concerns do you have about improving the situation?

☐ What do you think needs to be done?

☐ What training is needed?

☐ Specifically, how would that training help?

☐ Is there anyone else you think we should talk to?

Tips for writing effective questions

Effective questions save you work. Take time to structure them so that they elicit the best information for your needs.

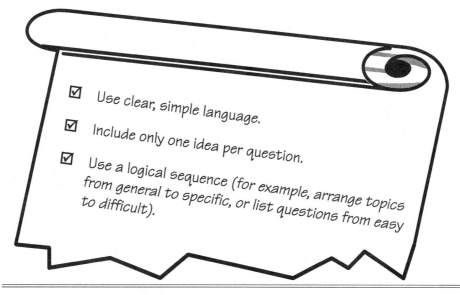

☑ Use clear, simple language.

☑ Include only one idea per question.

☑ Use a logical sequence (for example, arrange topics from general to specific, or list questions from easy to difficult).

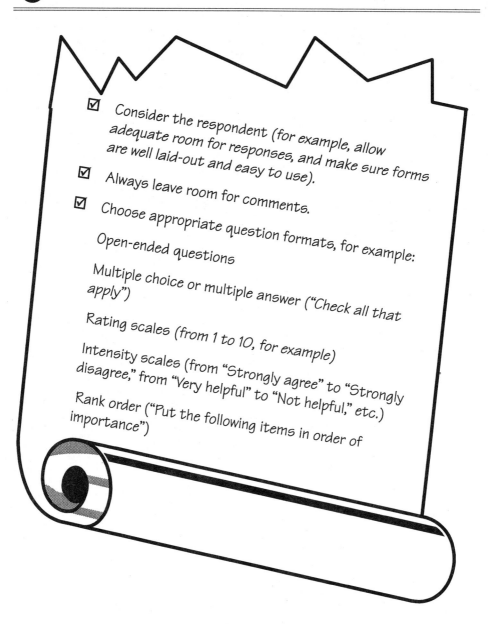

☑ Consider the respondent (for example, allow adequate room for responses, and make sure forms are well laid-out and easy to use).

☑ Always leave room for comments.

☑ Choose appropriate question formats, for example:

Open-ended questions

Multiple choice or multiple answer ("Check all that apply")

Rating scales (from 1 to 10, for example)

Intensity scales (from "Strongly agree" to "Strongly disagree," from "Very helpful" to "Not helpful," etc.)

Rank order ("Put the following items in order of importance")

How To Ask

There are endless ways to gather information, but for the purposes of a needs analysis, there are five frequently used methods you should consider. These methods are shown in the following Information-Gathering Methods chart:

	DESCRIPTION	**ADVANTAGES**	**CONSTRAINTS**	**TIPS**
Interviews *(in person and by telephone)*	One-on-one information gathering	Gets information directly Gets specific information Person feels heard Builds rapport Can read non-verbal messages	Takes time May not feel confidential Can be affected by interviewer's bias Can be difficult to organize	Send questions ahead Make a definite appointment *(even for phone interviews)*
Focus groups	Meetings of individuals who share an interest in the subject exchange Facilitated by a member of the information-gathering team	Good subjective information Creates an open atmosphere Participants piggyback on others' information	More anecdotal or subjective input Can be difficult to manage	Plan the mix for best results Use a short agenda Plan for convenience of participants; don't interrupt work flow
Surveys/ questionnaires	Information gathering on paper without the presence of an information gatherer	Reaches many people Confidential Quick Objective results Can be inexpensive	Return rate may be low People may not feel heard Communication is one way	Include a cover letter explaining why you are asking Provide clear instructions
Document analysis	Looking at existing documents and analyzing their effectiveness for the task	Provides background information without taking others' time Provides concrete examples Provides clues	Limited focus Can be time-consuming May not be many documents available	Use in combination with other methods Explain what you are doing Check annual reports, work samples, reports from department and teams
Observation	Watching people performing their jobs	Shows actual situation Does not take people away from the job Objective	People can change their behavior when *"watched"* All issues aren't subject to observation Time-consuming	Use with other methods Explain why you are there and what you are observing Be unobtrusive

Which method is best?

The method that gets you the information you need and is comfortable for you and for those you will be working with is the best method to use. You decide. Use one method or a combination of methods to best meet your needs.

In many cases, a variety is best. For example, you might use interviews for management, surveys and questionnaires with employees, and focus groups with customers—all in the same needs analysis. It really doesn't matter how many methods you employ; the important thing is to get the information you need in a timely and considerate manner.

Remember, whichever methods you use, you have a responsibility to tell the respondents how the information will be used and what information *(if any)* can remain confidential. If confidentiality is an issue for some respondents, you must respect that.

How will you gather and record data?

There is one other aspect of information gathering you should nail down before you begin. Make sure you develop a systematic approach to gather and record the data; that is, find a way to standardize the way information is captured. A computer program is ideal when you have personnel to input responses; but even if your budget won't permit this, make sure your information-gathering tool is organized. Use charts or questionnaires with space to write so that you can easily extract the information when you begin to analyze the results.

Prosperity Bank: Prospecting for Gold

At the next team meeting, Natalie filled the group in on her new assignment, showed them her charts of the current situation and the desired future state, and asked for their help. *"I have some ideas about what I think we need, but I'd like to get everyone's ideas about this. How about if I put together a one-page questionnaire that you could each fill out?"*

Most of the group agreed that this was a good approach. One holdout objected to doing the paperwork the questionnaire required, but the others cajoled her into participating. Natalie then asked if anyone in the group had other ideas for gathering information.

Josh volunteered immediately. *"I came from the telephone company, and we did a lot of cross-selling. I'd be happy to share with you some ideas I have."* Natalie and Josh decided to have lunch next week to talk about Josh's ideas.

Natalie then asked how she might reach those outside the group who have an impact on any plans the group might make. Dawn spoke up: *"One thing I notice is that we sometimes lose potential new customers because it takes too long to set up their accounts. I worked in operations a couple of years before I came to customer service. I'd be willing to talk to some of the operations people or the manager over there to see if they have any ideas for making things work more smoothly with new accounts. They may have some other ideas we can consider too."*

Natalie asked if anyone had a connection in marketing and would be willing to explore opportunities there. No one did, so Natalie said she would talk to Petra and then follow up with marketing herself.

Natalie promised to send the questionnaires to the group by the end of the week and asked to have them returned to her within five days. She also suggested that within the next week Dawn get in touch with operations and Natalie, in turn, promised to contact marketing. In this way, the project would continue to move forward. They all agreed that Natalie, Josh, and Dawn would meet after they had gathered the information and prepare a report to share at the next team meeting.

True to her word, Natalie distributed her questionnaire to the group by the end of the week. It looked like this:

1. What do you find easiest about cross-selling products and services?
   _____
   _____

2. What problems do you face in selling?
   _____
   _____

3. What kind of training would be useful to help you sell to customers?
   _____
   _____

4. Besides training, what else would be useful in helping you achieve management's goal for us?
   _____
   _____

5. What other ideas do you have that might help us with this issue?

In Dawn's interviews...

with operations and Natalie's with marketing, they explained what they were trying to achieve and the challenges they faced. They asked for specific ideas for overcoming these challenges and ways in which the groups could work more closely together to achieve customer satisfaction and improved profitability.

Summary

As with the first two actions of the needs analysis, you continue to use strategy in the information-gathering stage. You expand your existing partnerships by including key players as information gatherers or respondents. By involving others, you interest them in the outcome and continue to explore the larger picture.

You also consider your customers by devising a plan for asking a representative cross section of customers to contribute information.

CHAPTER SEVEN WORKSHEET: DESIGNING THE INFORMATION-GATHERING STAGE

WHOM SHOULD I ASK?	WHY THEM?	WHICH METHOD IS BEST?
Key players/ Management:		☐ Interviews ☐ Focus groups ☐ Surveys/questionnaires ☐ Document analysis ☐ Observation
Internal Customers:		☐ Interviews ☐ Focus groups ☐ Surveys/questionnaires ☐ Document analysis ☐ Observation
External Customers:		☐ Interviews ☐ Focus groups ☐ Surveys/questionnaires ☐ Document analysis ☐ Observation
Target Audience:		☐ Interviews ☐ Focus groups ☐ Surveys/questionnaires ☐ Document analysis ☐ Observation

WHO SHOULD DO THE ASKING?	WHY THEM?
Key players:	
Others:	

SORTING YOUR INFORMATION

Reviewing The Contributions

You have gathered all the information you think you need, and you are probably wondering, *"Now what do we do with it?"* Now you have to interpret the information to find out what it really tells you about your current situation and the challenges you face in moving to your future state. When you finish this step, you should have a document identifying the major training issues to be addressed and your recommendations for addressing them.

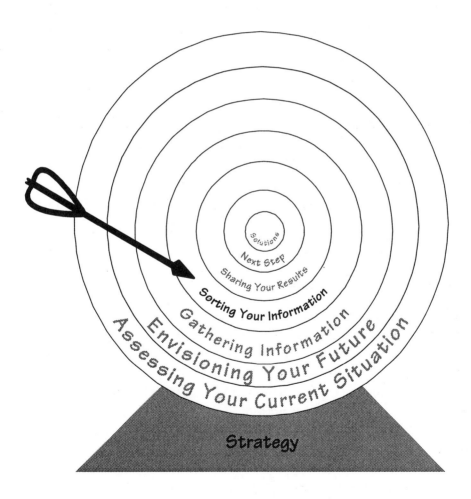

If you used a computerized information-gathering method, you can review the information quickly by providing it in any form you want. If you don't have a computer to assist you, you will have to organize and sort the  material yourself. Consider using a small team *(two or three people)* to independently review the information and identify issues. You can then meet and pool your findings. A team gives you a more objective analysis.

Identifying The Issues

Sorting the information into categories helps you manage it and identify themes and issues that must be addressed to reach your vision of the future.

When you sort your information into categories, you are looking for consistencies and connections between individual pieces of information. It may help you if you read through all your information once; then, as you begin to see comments repeated, you can jot down some possible categories to put them in. Some people like to highlight comments in different colors, with each color representing a different category. Then they can pick out all the yellow comments, for instance, group them together, and analyze their significance.

Prioritizing The Issues

Once you have organized the information into categories and looked at the significance of each contribution, you can begin to prioritize the issues. How you prioritize them depends on your specific situation. You might want to start with the category with the most comments, or you might want to start with the positive categories and then list the negative ones. Depending on your situation, it might be best to address the organization themes first and then the team themes or individual needs.

If you are analyzing numbers, you might prioritize the results by looking at the highest-rated item or the most frequent response.

Don't lose sight of your objective while you are doing the prioritizing. The importance of the issues should be directly related to achieving that desired future state.

Preparing The Information To Share With Others

You have sifted through the information, identified major categories, and considered your recommendations for moving ahead. Before you actually call a meeting or write a report to present your findings, you should spend some time preparing your presentation. Your goal in presenting the information is to have it acted upon, and a little preparation ahead of time will help you more easily achieve that goal.

As you think about developing your presentation, consider these two major design elements:

✓ Strategy

✓ Structure

Strategy

You have been using strategy throughout your needs analysis to involve others, consider the larger picture, and serve the customer. You can continue to do this here by inviting the key players to your feedback meeting and making sure the issues address both the larger picture and your internal and external customers' needs.

Another good strategy is to include positive statements about the current situation at the beginning of your presentation. People generally do the best they can, and you need to acknowledge that before you make recommendations to change the way things are done. You may also have among your key players a few people who constructed the methods you now need to change. If you want their support, you will need to exhibit a high degree of tact and sensitivity. Think about your material from their point of view, and organize it to help them.

Structure

The order in which you present your material and the topics you choose to present are also important to your success. Plan to explain your method for doing the needs analysis. This can be very brief if those present have been involved in the process from the beginning.

If the issues you intend to present are complex, consider developing an example to use with them to help clarify the information.

An important part of your presentation will be your recommendations. Keep them as open as possible, allowing for contributions from those present at the meeting. Vital information can come out in the feedback meeting. You will want to be able to address that situation if it comes up. By not carving your recommendations in stone, you allow yourself the flexibility to adjust them to new information.

RECOMMENDATIONS

Prosperity Bank: Collecting Nuggets

Natalie, Josh, and Dawn met to begin reviewing the information. They started with the questionnaires.

Several people said that many products had changed since the merger last year and that they didn't feel they understood the new products well enough to recommend them to customers. People were also confused by other changes in the organization, such as the relocation of branches. It was becoming difficult to remember where the ATMs were, so how could you pass this information on to customers? Some of the people in operations had also changed, so it was harder to follow up when a customer had a problem with a statement. One respondent asked, "*If we can't address a customer's problems, how can we convince them to buy even more products or services?*"

Several people mentioned that the sales training given last year was interesting but didn't address one of their primary needs—smoothly turning a service call into a sales call. Respondents were also concerned about answering calls quickly. *"Adding sales to service means more time on the phone. While we are talking to one customer, other customers are piling up in the queue,"* one rep said.

Feeling slightly overwhelmed, the team turned from the questionnaires to the information Josh had shared with Natalie at lunch. Josh said that on his old job, each rep had a three-ring binder with a tab for each type of product or service. Behind each tab were separate pages for each product or service, listing key features and benefits, prices, answers to typical customer questions, and the types of customers the items were designed for. The notebooks made it easy for reps to flip to the right page during a phone call and have all the information they needed right in front of them.

Josh also mentioned staff meetings where everyone shared ideas about problems they had encountered with customers. Sometimes they role-played solving a particular problem or talking to a customer about a new product.

Dawn reported that the biggest problem operations had was that sometimes the rep didn't fill out all the spaces on the New Account form. Operations would then have to call the rep *(or worse, the customer)* to get the needed information. Sometimes the customer's name or address was misspelled, and the customer would get angry.

Operations also complained that the reps would call about a situation and act as if operations were at fault. Sometimes, the reps would get really nasty on the phone. Dawn reported that one person she talked to said, *"Our workload has gone up 30 percent since the merger, and we haven't been able to add any additional staff. When a rep starts complaining about the job we do, we get angry too. After all, we are also trying to do a good job for the customer."*

Dawn told Natalie and Josh that one operations employee had volunteered to talk to the reps and explain the forms and the problems.

Natalie then added the information from marketing. It wasn't much. The marketing person had been really busy and said changes to product and service information were the retail division's responsibility, not marketing's. He said that there were so many changes that half the time he didn't know what was out there. He added that it would probably get worse if the merger with another bank, currently being discussed, actually happened.

The team felt overwhelmed. Somehow they had to organize this material into a simple format that could be shared at the staff meeting. From their initial review, they decided that there were four categories:

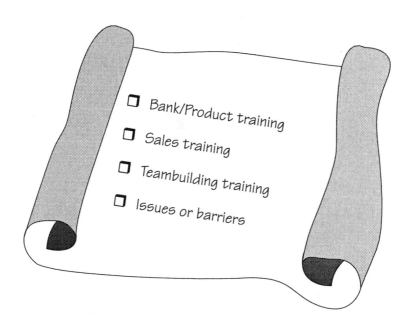

☐ Bank/Product training

☐ Sales training

☐ Teambuilding training

☐ Issues or barriers

They made a chart and summarized the information as shown below:

TRAINING NEEDS SUMMARY CHART

BANK/PRODUCT TRAINING	SALES TRAINING	TEAMBUILDING TRAINING	ISSUES OR BARRIERS
Products/branches change	How to move a call from service to sales	How to get answers from operations	Sales calls take time; customers pile up in the queue
Product knowledge	How to probe for customer need	Accuracy of New Account form for operations	Time constraints (everybody's already burdened)
Three-ring binder of products/services	How to assess customer's desire for help	Reps' attitude toward operations	Further changes may be coming in future
Key phrases to help customer understand benefits of products and services	What questions to ask to uncover customer needs	Marketing too busy to contribute	
	Staff meeting role-playing	Operations to talk to group about forms and problems	

Once they organized the issues onto a chart, they all felt better. This was a manageable list.

There is no set format for presenting the results of your information gathering. Choose a method that works for you and that you are comfortable with. Another format for organizing information by skills, knowledge, and attitudes is included in the Appendix labeled *"Charting The Training Need."*

Summary

Sorting your information is at the heart of your needs analysis. By condensing the raw data into some kind of manageable form and then interpreting it, you begin to develop the recommendations. Many times, you discover that the solution requires more than training. Natalie, Josh, and Dawn discovered that the changing nature of their organization and the burdens already placed on the staff will have an impact on their solutions. Natalie's team also uncovered concerns about the lack of advance information from marketing and the *"pass-the-buck"* attitudes of marketing and retail. Andy faced this same situation when he discovered that the forms did not match the computer screens used to enter data. You should discuss these non-training issues when you share your results.

In some cases, your information may indicate that the issues that need to be addressed are not training issues at all. If this happens, you still share the information, but the last two steps in the needs analysis process *(sharing your results and deciding your next step)* will focus on non-training action plans.

Interpreting the information is not an easy process. You must use both your intellect and your perceptions to develop useful recommendations. Of course, you may get additional ideas when you present your findings to others so keep your recommendations flexible enough to allow for further contributions.

CHAPTER EIGHT WORKSHEET: CHARTING THE ISSUES

 Use the following worksheet to categorize and chart the major issues raised and to list examples of these issues.

ISSUES			

EXAMPLES

SHARING YOUR RESULTS

When you share your results with others, your goal is to present the information in a way that will move you forward. Your assessment should be positive and encouraging. Offer hope for actions to address needs, and be prepared with recommendations to share as well. There are two things to consider when you share results with others:

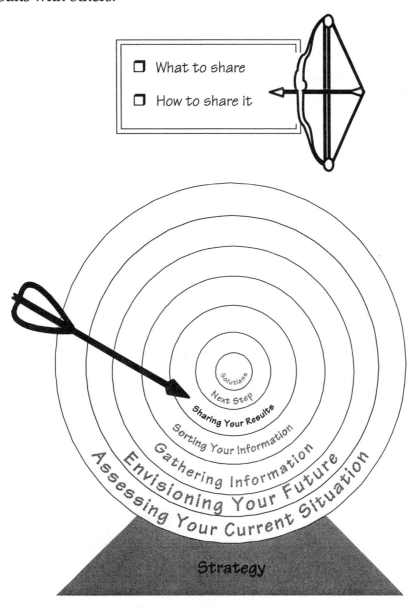

☐ What to share

☐ How to share it

Solutions

Next Step

Sharing Your Results

Sorting Your Information

Gathering Information

Envisioning Your Future

Assessing Your Current Situation

Strategy

What To Share

Planning what you will share with others assures that you won't forget a vital piece of information or an explanation that will persuade others of the need to move forward. There are six steps in sharing your results with others:

☑ Describe your needs analysis method

☑ Present your information

☑ Identify issues

☑ Listen and absorb the reaction

☑ Discuss the reaction

☑ Present recommendations

Describe your method

If you have been working with a small group, your method may already be familiar to all those involved. If this is the case, you can skip this step or discuss your method very briefly.

If, however, you are sharing results with individuals who are not familiar with your method, review the needs analysis process you are using. Give a short history of the need for the project and how you got to this point. This is also a good time to thank them for their contributions to the project and for their ongoing support.

Present your information

Participants will be more attentive to your conclusions if they understand how you developed them. By discussing some of the raw information you received, you involve the group and gain their understanding and support. You  might want to quote some of the respondents directly if their comments are particularly powerful or telling. Consider sharing information about the most frequent response or the most positive one—whatever will help impress upon people the need to move ahead.

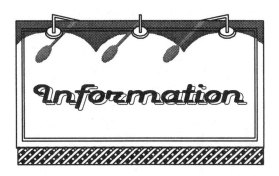

Identify the issues

This is where you present your analysis of the raw information and identify the key issues to be addressed. You can add your own insights and observations to this material if you think it will help, but avoid making recommendations at this point. People need time to absorb the analysis before they are ready to consider ways to address the issues.

If you can link the issues to management concerns or organization objectives, by all means do so; it will strengthen your presentation. Also, if some of the findings support an intuition shared with you early in the process, make sure you credit the person whose intuition has now been proven correct by the facts. You will create a staunch ally by doing so.

Listen to and absorb the reaction

This is probably the hardest part of sharing the results. You have done all this research, you have crafted an analysis of the key issues, and now you have to wait for and manage the reaction.

If your group has been involved throughout the process, the reaction should be very supportive and positive. After all, there are no surprises in the information you present. If, however, the information is new to some individuals, it may take them a while to digest it and respond.

Discuss the reaction

If the silence becomes oppressive, you can encourage a response by selecting one topic and probing for more information about it. For example, if your investigation showed that employees need clearer communication from management, ask one of your management key players what information is currently communicated. The purpose of asking is to start 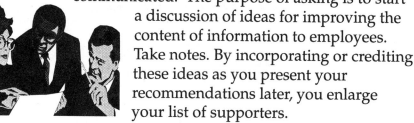 a discussion of ideas for improving the content of information to employees. Take notes. By incorporating or crediting these ideas as you present your recommendations later, you enlarge your list of supporters.

Present recommendations

Presenting your recommendations is less a distinct step and more a continuation of the discussion of ideas. You can guide the process or summarize an idea by supplying your recommendations as they become relevant to the discussion. You can also present your recommendations as a way to focus the discussion if it begins to drift or unravel.

The goal of presenting and discussing recommendations is to develop a firm list of ideas for addressing the situation you started with. In guiding the discussion, you have the responsibility of ensuring that all major training issues are addressed by specific recommendations.

How To Share

What to share is the challenging part; but how to share is also
important. Remember to be positive and encouraging. Use every
opportunity to draw support from the group and to credit their
contributions.

Be objective when presenting the actual information from your
investigation. Think of yourself as a witness and report accurately.
Save your insights or ideas until after you have identified the
issues.

Consider using visuals or charts to support your information. It
gives those present another way to interpret what you are saying.
Examples and metaphors can also help your audience understand
the material.

Be sure to have the raw information available as backup. Someone
might ask to see those interviews, questionnaires, or whatever else
you used to get to this point in the needs analysis. Having it readily
available is another way to demonstrate the strength of your
process.

Prosperity Bank: Sharing the Wealth

Natalie, Josh, and Dawn took their information analysis to the team meeting. Because Petra is a key player in the needs analysis, she was invited to attend the meeting as well.

Natalie, Josh, and Dawn agreed beforehand that Natalie would present the results. Natalie started by briefly reviewing the method they used and reporting on some of the raw information from the questionnaires. She also reported briefly on the meetings with operations and marketing. She told them about Josh's three-ring notebook idea, and she used their chart to present the issues.

Before turning the meeting over to a group discussion of the issues, Natalie pointed out the following positive observations from the information gathering:

☐ The reps have a definite customer focus. They understand customer needs, and they want to help fulfill them.

☐ The reps are committed to Prosperity Bank and have years of solid experience with banking issues.

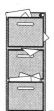

The positive remarks were well received by the group.

Josh's notebook idea also generated immediate interest. One of the reps said: *"I have stuff all over my desk and in a couple of drawers. Sometimes I'm not sure what's new and what's out of date. Having it all in the same format and in a single notebook would really help."*

Another rep said: *"I wonder if the reps in the branches have the same problem we do. Maybe they would like to have something like this if they don't already."*

When the discussion turned to the information from marketing, Kai, one of the reps, got upset. *"This is an even bigger problem than I wrote about in my questionnaire,"* she said. When she didn't elaborate, Petra encouraged her by saying: *"I've heard comments about marketing from others as well. I'd really be interested in hearing about your experience. Will you share it with us? Perhaps we can find a solution."*

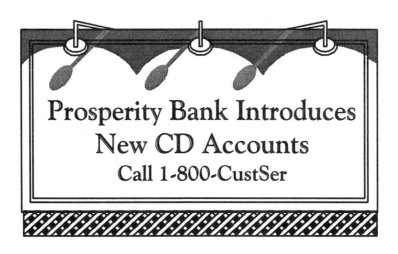

Prosperity Bank Introduces
New CD Accounts
Call 1-800-CustSer

Kai continued: *"I've had customers ask me about changes in products I've never heard of. One time, I asked the customer where he heard about this product, and he told me there was a billboard advertising it near the freeway. I checked it out on my way home, and there is was—big as life—this billboard about the new CD accounts, listing our customer service number for more information. You'd think if they had time to put up a billboard, they would have had time to fill us in. It was a whole week later before I got anything in writing about these new accounts."*

When Natalie mentioned that marketing had told her to go to retail for product information, Petra explained that marketing and retail had a history of turf issues. *"Perhaps we've touched a nerve over this issue. Let me talk to Hans, the VP of retail, and see how we can resolve the situation,"* Petra suggested.

Another rep volunteered that he felt uncomfortable selling to customers. *"I was hired to be a service rep, and I'm good at helping people. Now, I'm being asked to push products on our customers,"* he explained. Petra asked if the other reps had similar feelings. The majority indicated they did.

"We're moving so fast to stay in business," Petra said, *"that we haven't had time to think about the training and information you need. A survey of our customers shows that they want more help with financial issues and would welcome our assistance. In fact, there's a film of customer interviews that marketing put together that shows this. Maybe I could get someone from marketing to come and share what our customers have said. It sounds as if we need to provide some training on how describing our products and services can meet customer needs."*

Natalie realized that she had not investigated the needs of her external customers as part of the information gathering. She is relieved to find out that marketing has this information to share.

Natalie noted the areas of concern from the discussion and added them to the chart.

Bank/Product Training	Sales Training	Teambuilding Training	Issues or Barriers
Products/branches change	How to move a call from service to sales	How to get answers from operations	Sales calls take time; customers pile up in the queue
Product knowledge	How to probe for customer need	Accuracy of New Account form for operations	Time constraints (everybody's already burdened)
three-ring binder of products/services	How to assess customer's desire for help	Reps' attitude toward operations	Further changes may be coming in future
Key phrases to help customer understand benefits of products and services	What questions to ask to uncover customer needs	Marketing too busy to contribute	Marketing/retail turf issues
No advance information on new products or services	Staff meeting role-playing	Operations to talk to group about forms and problems	
	Being pushy; not helping		
	Marketing to talk to reps about customer needs		

Using the issues from their chart, group members came up with several specific recommendations, including:

☒ Develop sales training for the reps

☒ Develop bank/product training

☒ Develop teambuilding training

☒ Resolve the issues and barriers to effective training

The group was satisfied with the recommendations, and Petra was very impressed. She asked them to come up with an action plan within the next week for implementing the recommendations.

Summary

Sharing the results with others and developing the recommendations for action can be a heady experience. You suddenly begin to see the fruits of your efforts, and everyone is energized to address the situation and improve it.

It is in this stage of the needs analysis that you can see the results of your strategy. You have a focused team of individuals ready to move forward on the issues. You have included the key players in your feedback event, and both organization issues and customer issues are addressed.

The momentum you create in sharing the results should carry you right into your action planning.

CHAPTER NINE WORKSHEET:
SUMMARY SHEET FOR SHARING RESULTS

Use this worksheet to organize your presentation and remind yourself of where you are in the process.

The Method Used	• _____ _____ _____
Key Information To Share	• _____ • _____ • _____
Issues	• _____ • _____ • _____
Listen*	
Discuss Issues*	
Possible Recommendations	• _____ • _____ • _____
Final Recommendations*	

*Leave blank to capture contributions from others

DECIDING YOUR NEXT STEP

The last action in the needs analysis process is to translate the recommendations into a plan of action. You are creating a list of activities that will be used in the next phase of the High-IMPACT Training Model—Mapping the Training Approach.

You are not actually doing the design of training in this last action. You are simply creating a description of the specific training required to improve the situation. You are also assigning responsibility for doing activities to specific individuals and establishing a due date for completion. This action ensures that the work done to date is not wasted and that the project continues to move forward.

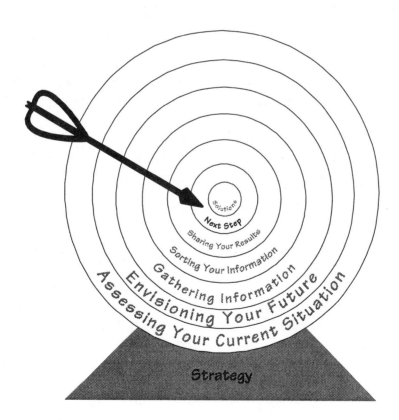

There are three key elements to a successful action plan:

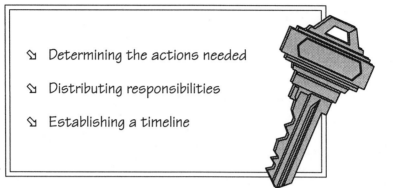

↘ Determining the actions needed

↘ Distributing responsibilities

↘ Establishing a timeline

Determining The Actions Needed

The recommendations are your starting point for developing the actions needed. If they are not currently worded as actions, rewrite them so they are. Be sure that everyone understands what is to be accomplished by each action and that everyone is in agreement.

You may want to decide on the approach you will use for the training *(computer-based training, instructor-based training, job aids, etc.)* and whether or not you will use internal or external sources.

Distributing The Responsibilities

Each action in your action plan should be assigned to a specific person. It would be even better if you had volunteers. Even if a team will be performing the task, record the name of one person on the team as the contact and the person responsible for the team's activities.

Establishing A Timeline

For each action item, establish a due date for completion of the task. A due date gives participants a target and helps them focus their activities toward results.

Putting the action steps, the person responsible, and the due dates on a chart for everyone to use will help keep the project moving forward and will provide you with a way to check on progress. Someone has to keep the momentum going; and as the leader of the needs analysis, you get the job. Determining what needs to be done is just the first phase.

Prosperity Bank: Collecting Dividends

Using the chart of recommendations, Natalie and her group created their action plan.

ACTION	PERSON RESPONSIBLE	DUE DATE	NEXT STEP
Develop product/service training	Josh	April 1	Talk to branches to determine current training used
Develop sales training	Natalie	May 1	Review previous sales training and talk to vendor
Develop teambuilding training	Dawn	June 1	Set up a meeting with operations to discuss ways to work more cooperatively
Resolve issues and address barriers	Petra	May 1	Explore with Hans the marketing/retail issue

In effect, the TCSD Training Action Plan establishes the development teams for the training issues and identifies the team leaders. The team leaders can now begin Phase 2 of the High-IMPACT Training Model, Mapping the Training Approach. In the mapping phase, team leaders and their teams will develop measurable objectives for the training and a design plan to meet the training needs, using the information and ideas from the needs analysis.

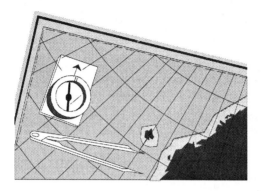

Identifying targeted training needs has now been completed, but before moving on to the next phase, Natalie takes a moment to see how her needs analysis process helped her gather the information she needed to hit the target. She develops this summary:

An Effective Needs Analysis Tells You . . .	TCSD's Action Plan Told Them . . .
Where the target is	The target is to help customer service reps improve their ability to sell by providing training and support.
How large the target is	The target was larger than just TCSD. It needed to include marketing, retail, and operations and an understanding of customer needs.
How far away the target is	The target was within range of TCSD's staff. It was *"doable."*
What kind of arrows to use	Training was needed in the areas of: • Sales skills • Product/service knowledge • Teambuilding • Cross-functional cooperation and understanding
Who should shoot the arrows	Training should be done by: • Team leaders for the various training development teams • Key people from marketing, retail, and operations • Reps themselves sharing ideas during training and at staff meetings
When to shoot	Competition dictates immediately. The action plan is set up to start the process rolling now.
About dangerous crosscurrents	Marketing and retail have a history of rivalry Everyone's time to help is limited More changes in the organization are likely

▌ TCSD has done a good job and is now in a position to move forward.

Summary

Developing an action plan completes the needs analysis phase and feeds the next phase of the High-IMPACT Training Model. The action plan assures that you will keep moving forward. It assigns responsibility for the training to specific individuals and gives them a timeline for completing the identified actions.

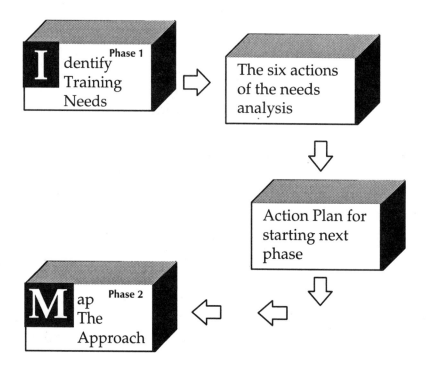

CHAPTER TEN WORKSHEET:
THE ACTION PLAN

 Use this worksheet to zero in on the key actions and next steps in your needs assessment.

ACTION	PERSON RESPONSIBLE	DUE DATE	NEXT STEP

CHAPTER ELEVEN

SUMMARY

Now is the time for a celebration of your achievement. You have completed the first phase of the High-IMPACT Training Model and have set yourself up for the next phase—Mapping the Training Approach.

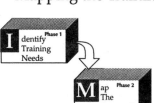

You have worked through the six actions necessary to identify and target your training needs:

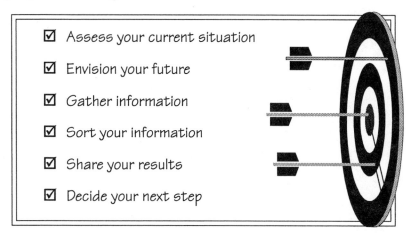

☑ Assess your current situation

☑ Envision your future

☑ Gather information

☑ Sort your information

☑ Share your results

☑ Decide your next step

The end products of your efforts are a description of the training needed and an action plan for beginning Phase 2, Mapping the Training Approach.

At each step in the process, you have used good strategy to establish a partnership with others, consider the larger picture, and serve the customer.

You have hit your target accurately using both your needs analysis skills and your intelligence; and you have provided direction and content to keep the training project moving forward. Congratulations!

REPRODUCIBLE FORMS
AND WORKSHEETS

The pages in the Appendix are provided for you to photocopy and use appropriately.

USING STRATEGY TO CONTRIBUTE TO ORGANIZATION GROWTH

Use the following questions to guide your strategy for identifying targeted training needs.

The Larger Picture

1. What is the vision of your organization? Where does your organization want to go?

_____

_____

_____

_____

_____

2. What is the mission of your organization? What is its purpose for existing?

_____

_____

_____

_____

_____

3. What are the business objectives of your organization?

_____

_____

_____

_____

_____

_____

_____

_____

Working in Partnership

4. What other areas or departments do you interact with?

_____

_____

_____

_____

_____

_____

_____

_____

5. Whom should you involve? Who is critical to your success?

_____

_____

_____

_____

_____

_____

Serving the Customer

6. Who are your internal and your external customers?

_____

_____

_____

_____

_____

_____

_____

CURRENT SITUATION WORKSHEET

Where are we now?

Why do we think we need training?

What organization issues are driving the need for training?

ENVISIONING THE FUTURE

Where do we want to be?

What would success look like?

Do we have the whole picture?

DESIGNING THE INFORMATION-GATHERING STAGE

WHOM SHOULD I ASK?	WHY THEM?	WHICH METHOD IS BEST?
Key players/ Management:		☐ Interviews ☐ Focus groups ☐ Surveys/questionnaires ☐ Document analysis ☐ Observation
Internal Customers:		☐ Interviews ☐ Focus groups ☐ Surveys/questionnaires ☐ Document analysis ☐ Observation
External Customers:		☐ Interviews ☐ Focus groups ☐ Surveys/questionnaires ☐ Document analysis ☐ Observation
Target Audience:		☐ Interviews ☐ Focus groups ☐ Surveys/questionnaires ☐ Document analysis ☐ Observation

DESIGNING THE INFORMATION-GATHERING STAGE
(cont.)

WHO SHOULD DO THE ASKING?	WHY THEM?
Key players:	
Others:	

CHARTING THE ISSUES

ISSUES			

EXAMPLES

CHARTING THE TRAINING NEED

One method to capture the results of your information gathering is to sort the information into the following categories:

☑ Skills *(both existing skills and needed ones)*

☑ Knowledge *(both existing knowledge and required knowledge)*

☑ Attitudes *(both existing ones and desired future attitudes)*

This approach works best when a definite training need exists, and the questions in the information-gathering step are crafted to explore these specific categories.

GROUP	SKILLS	KNOWLEDGE	ATTITUDES	OTHER FACTORS
A				
B				
C				
D				

SUMMARY SHEET FOR SHARING RESULTS

Use this worksheet to organize your presentation and to remind you of where you are in the process.

The Method Used	• _____ _____ _____
Key Information To Share	• _____ • _____ • _____
Issues	• _____ • _____ • _____
Listen*	
Discuss Issues*	
Possible Recommendations	• _____ • _____ • _____
Final Recommendations*	

*Leave blank to capture contributions from others

THE ACTION PLAN

ACTION	PERSON RESPONSIBLE	DUE DATE	NEXT STEP

THE PRACTICAL GUIDEBOOK COLLECTION FROM RICHARD CHANG ASSOCIATES, INC. PUBLICATIONS DIVISION

Our Practical Guidebook Collection is growing to meet the challenges of the ever-changing workplace of the 90's. Look for these and other titles from Richard Chang Associates, Inc. on your bookstore shelves and in book catalogs.

QUALITY IMPROVEMENT SERIES

- Meetings That Work!
- Continuous Improvement Tools Volume 1
- Continuous Improvement Tools Volume 2
- Step-By-Step Problem Solving
- Satisfying Internal Customers First!
- Continuous Process Improvement
- Improving Through Benchmarking
- Succeeding As A Self-Managed Team
- Reengineering In Action

MANAGEMENT SKILLS SERIES

- Coaching Through Effective Feedback
- Expanding Leadership Impact
- Mastering Change Management
- On-The-Job Orientation And Training
- Recreating Teams During Transitions

HIGH PERFORMANCE TEAM SERIES

- Success Through Teamwork
- Team Decision-Making Techniques
- Measuring Team Performance
- Building A Dynamic Team

HIGH-IMPACT TRAINING SERIES

- Creating High-Impact Training
- Identifying Targeted Training Needs
- Applying Successful Training Techniques
- Measuring The Impact Of Training
- Make Your Training Results Last

ADDITIONAL RESOURCES
FROM RICHARD CHANG ASSOCIATES, INC.

Improve your training sessions and seminars with the ideal tools—videos from Richard Chang Associates, Inc. You and your team will easily relate to the portrayals of real-life workplace situations. You can apply our innovative techniques to your own situations for immediate results.

TRAINING VIDEOTAPES

Mastering Change Management*
Turning Obstacles Into Opportunities

Step-By-Step Problem Solving*
A Practical Approach To Solving Problems On The Job

Quality: You Don't Have To Be Sick To Get Better**
Individuals Do Make a Difference

Achieving Results Through Quality Improvement**

*Authored by Dr. Richard Chang and produced by Double Vision Studios.
**Produced by American Media Inc. in conjunction with Richard Chang Associates, Inc.
 Each video includes a Facilitator's Guide.

"THE HUMAN EDGE SERIES" VIDEOTAPES

Total Quality: Myths, Methods, Or Miracles
Featuring Drs. Ken Blanchard and Richard Chang

Empowering The Quality Effort
Featuring Drs. Ken Blanchard and Richard Chang

Produced by Double Vision Studios.

"THE TOTAL QUALITY SERIES"
TRAINING VIDEOTAPES AND WORKBOOKS

Building Commitment *(Telly Award Winner)*
How To Build Greater Commitment To Your TQ Efforts

Teaming Up
How To Successfully Participate On Quality-Improvement Teams

Applied Problem Solving
How To Solve Problems As An Individual Or On A Team

Self-Directed Evaluation
How To Establish Feedback Methods To Self-Monitor Improvements

Authored by Dr. Richard Chang and produced by Double Vision Studios, each videotape from *"The Total Quality Series"* includes a *Facilitator's Guide* and five *Participant Workbooks* with each purchase. Additional *Participant Workbooks* are available for purchase.

EVALUATION AND FEEDBACK FORM

We need your help to continuously improve the quality of the resources provided through the Richard Chang Associates, Inc., Publications Division. We would greatly appreciate your input and suggestions regarding this particular guidebook, as well as future guidebook interests.

Please photocopy this form before completing it, since other readers may use this guidebook. Thank you in advance for your feedback.

Guidebook Title: _____

1. Overall, how would you rate your *level of satisfaction* with this guidebook? Please circle your response.

    Extremely Dissatisfied   Satisfied   Extremely Satisfied

            1   2   3   4   5

2. What specific *concepts or methods* did you find <u>most</u> helpful?

    _____

    _____

3. What specific *concepts or methods* did you find <u>least</u> helpful?

    _____

    _____

4. As an individual who may purchase additional guidebooks in the future, what *characteristics/features/benefits* are most important to you in making a decision to purchase a guidebook *(or another similar book)*?

    _____

    _____

5. What additional *subject matter/topic areas* would you like to see addressed in future guidebooks?

    _____

    _____

Name *(optional)*: _____

Address: _____

C/S/Z: _____ **Phone (   )** _____